Published by:
Sam Kaura
225 – 1717 – 60 ST. SE
Calgary, Alberta
Canada T2A 7Y7
E-Mail: abcofsuccess@gmail.com

Cover design by Amit Malhotra

ISBN 0-7795-0159-4

Printed by:
Blitz Print
3, 1235 – 64 AVE. SE
Calgary, Alberta
Canada T2H 2J7

Advance Praise for ABC Of Success

"A small book with awesome power, that needs to be in everyone's hand. It will unlock the hidden talents we all have and has a very potent emotional Payoff."

- Walter Koenig, Auto Fix

"This book has changed my life for the best. I am living by 'Law Of Choice' now than 'Law Of Accident'."

- Amit Malhotra, Amit Printing Press

"The ABC Of Success is a great book, really gets to the point. This book lays the foundation to start setting goals for the future."

- Marilyn Bonas, Nursing Supervisor

"This book should be required reading for all the students in the schools."

- Mark Bagai, Payless Travel

“This book is very valuable for people to set up & achieve their goals.”

- Dr E. Laifer

“A great book to turn goals into reality.”

- Durgesh Malhotra, Nursing Student

“A simple book to achieve your goals.”

- Rajibe Razi, Realtor

“It is a very valuable book for everybody to achieve whatever they want out of their life.”

Michael Remezof, Farmer

Dedication

This book is dedicated to you, 'The most important person.'

Acknowledgements

I am thankful to my family, my parents; Mr. and Mrs. W.C. Kaura, my wife; Cecilia, my sons; Sony and Rana, daughter; Gita, son-in-law; Chad Evans and daughter-in-law; Durgesh (Khushi). Our contributing friends; Dr. E. Laifer, Barry and Carol Martin, Marilyn Bonas, Diane Bonas, Keith Davidson, Michael Remezoff, Aischaa Luuri, Tash Khimani, Walter Koenig, Mahesh Kavia, Rajeeb Razi, Bruce McMullin, Kewal and Narinder Dhugga, Thomas Tom and Dr. Salim Aziz.

"You want to be famous, successful, winner, you have to be VISIONARY."

Table of Contents

PROLOGUE: BEGINNING OF A NEW JOURNEY - VISION

John and his cousin Jill were in the same junior high school, were both honor students, belonged to middle class families and both wanted to be medical doctors. After twenty years, John was an elementary school teacher and Jill was a very successful medical doctor with her own private practice. Jill had more wealth than the combined wealth of the rest of her junior high school class. The reason for this was because Jill was living by the law of choice and John was living by the law of accident. Jill had her written goals and she did her daily visualization to achieve whatever she wanted in her life. On the other hand, John has no written goals, did not do daily visualization and lived by the law of accident. Now you have the choice to either live by the law of choice or the law of accident. It is all up to you. In this book you will learn how to live by the law of choice.

It is all up to you to be successful in life. Your life is in your own hands. You can live by the law of choice instead by the law of accident.

Your life is just like a car. When you drive a car you usually have a destination in mind and you usually reach that destination. Even if the car breaks down on the way you will still reach your destination although you might be late. Similarly, in your life, once you have a VISION STATEMENT (what you want to be), GOALS and a BURNING DESIRE, FAITH AND FOCUS, you will achieve your destination. In this book you will learn how you can steer your life on whatever course you want.

One day, my five-year-old daughter went to her friend's house without telling us. We looked all over for her. Finally, when she came home, I asked her, "Where did you go, Nancy?"

"I went to my friend's house." She said.

"Why did you go there without telling us?" I asked.

"I just went by accident, Dad." She replied.

We can relate to this story because most of us are living by the LAW OF ACCIDENT so when good things happen, we call it good luck and when bad things happen, we call it bad luck. By failing to plan we plan to fail and keep living by the LAW OF ACCIDENT instead of the LAW OF CHOICE.

Let me share with you another story from the Internet by an anonymous author.

"YOU HAVE TWO CHOICES"

Jerry is the manager of a restaurant and is always in a GOOD mood.

When someone would ask him, "How are

you doing?" he would always reply, "If I were any better I would be twins."
When he changed his job many of the waiters and waitresses at his restaurant quit their job so they could follow him.

They followed him **because Jerry was a <u>natural motivator</u>.**

If an employee was having a bad day, Jerry was always trying to help him or her look on the positive side of the situation. Seeing this style really made me curious, so one day I went up to Jerry and asked him, "I don't get it! No one can be positive all of the time. How do you do it?"
Jerry replied, "Each morning I wake up and say to myself that I have two choices today. I can choose to be in a good mood or choose to be in bad mood. I always choose to be in a good mood. Each time something bad happens I can choose to be a victim or I can choose to learn from it. I always choose to learn from it. Every time someone comes to me complaining, I can

choose to accept his or her complaint or I can point out the positive side of life. I always choose the positive side of life."

"But, it's not always that easy." I protested.

"Yes it is." Jerry said. "Life is always choices. When you cut away all the junk every situation is a choice".

Several years later, I heard that Jerry accidentally did something you're not supposed to do in the restaurant business. He left the back door of his restaurant open, and in the morning, three armed men robbed him.

While Jerry was trying to open the safe his hand, shaking from nervousness, slipped off the combination. The robbers panicked and shot him. Luckily Jerry was found quickly and rushed to the hospital. After eighteen hours of surgery and weeks of intensive care, Jerry was released from the hospital with fragments of the bullets still in his body. I saw Jerry about six months after the accident and when I asked him how he was, he replied,

"If I were any better, I would be twins. Want to see my scars?"

I declined to see his wounds but did ask him what had gone through his mind as the robbery took place.

"The first thing that went through my mind was that I should have locked the back door." Jerry replied.

"Then after they shot me, as I lay on the floor, I remembered that I had two choices, I could choose to live or I could choose to die. I chose to live."

"Were you not scared?" I asked.

Jerry continued, "The paramedics were great. They kept telling me. I was going to be fine. But when they wheeled me into the emergency room and I saw the expressions on the face of the doctors and nurses, I got really scared. In their eyes I read, "He's a dead man." I knew I needed to take action."

"What did you do?" I asked.

"Well there was a big nurse shouting questions at me" said Jerry. "She asked if I was allergic to anything."

"Yes. To bullets", I replied.

Over their laughter I told them, "I'm choosing to live. Please operate on me as if I am alive, not dead."

Jerry lived thanks to the skill of his doctors but also because of his '**AMAZING ATTITUDE**.'

I learned from him that everyday you have the choice to either enjoy your life or hate it.

The only thing that's truly yours, that no one can control or take from you – is your **ATTITUDE**.

So if you can take care of that, everything else in life becomes much easier.

Here is another formula we live by: Outcome is the Result of your Reaction to a Situation.

SITUATION + REACTION = OUTCOME

You cannot change the situation but you can change your reaction to the situation and by reacting in a positive way you can change the outcome.

Whatever happens in our life is governed by two natural laws: the Law of accident and the Law of choice. We get fifty thousand thoughts daily, positive or negative. When thoughts come by accident we live by the law of accident. When we feed ourselves with positive thoughts we live by the law of choice. Therefore let's start living by the law of choice.

Start feeding your mind with positive thoughts. You know that **GIGO** means Garbage In, Garbage Out. When you feed yourself with negative thoughts, it will result in negative situations in your life, and when you nourish yourself with positive thoughts, the results will naturally be positive.

In the above story, Jerry was shot in a robbery but his reaction was positive. He made the choice to live. He thought he was **LUCKY** to be alive. He did not think that he was unlucky because he got shot. His positive attitude changed the outcome from death to life.

There was an article in the June 2004 issue of Reader's Digest called, "How to Get Lucky: New **SCIENTIFIC** Proof That You Make Your Own Breaks" by Richard Wiseman.

By changing your Attitude–expecting good fortune rather than dwelling on bad fortune–your Bad LUCK may vanish. In the case of Bad Luck (Situation), deal by imagining that things could be worse. In his studies, when people dealt with bad things by imagining them to be worse, 80 percent were happier and more satisfied with their life and felt luckier after only one month.

In case of robbery as in Jerry's story, unlucky people would say it was their bad luck to be in that robbery, but lucky people would say, "It could have been worse. I could have died on the spot." This kind of thinking, like Jerry had, makes us feel better about ourselves, keeps expectations high and increases the likelihood of continuing to live a Positive and Lucky life.

You may have heard that you are the composite of the five people you associate with the most. I am sure you have heard, "A man is known by the company he keeps," so the choice is yours. Do you want to **GRUB** with the **TURKEYS** or **FLY** with **Eagles**? This book is for those of you who want to FLY WITH THE EAGLES. You are born as a Star and you can shine as a star. I am sure you want to be a Star otherwise you will not be reading this book.

Let us do a quick quiz now:

There are three words, HAVE, DO & BE, there are six combinations of these words, which are as follows:

1	**2**	**3**	**4**	**5**	**6**
HAVE	HAVE	DO	DO	BE	BE
BE	DO	BE	HAVE	DO	HAVE
DO	BE	HAVE	BE	HAVE	DO

Let me explain to you the first combination:

HAVE
BE
DO

There are lots of people who want to HAVE (ex. lots of money) first, so that they can BE (ex. rich) and DO whatever they want to do with the money (ex. buying cars, houses, etc.)
Did you hear the song, "If I Had a Million Dollars"? First he wants to HAVE a million dollars and then he will BE somebody important and DO the things he wants to do.
Think of all these combinations and figure out which is the best combination to be successful in life. The answer is on the next page.

The best answer is: **<u>BE, DO, and HAVE</u>**

BE—Decide what you want to BE first—your vision statement.

DO—Do whatever you have to DO to be that person—action plan.

HAVE—HAVE comes automatically.

You know most of us buy lottery tickets and most never win. Now you know why, because we are taking one of the incorrect formulas:

HAVE		HAVE
DO	or	BE
BE		DO

Let us start practicing the **"<u>BE + DO + HAVE</u>"** formula. First of all we have to start living by law of choice not by law of accident. To do that, lets start writing our vision statement. Right now.

One of my vision statements is "I have a great day." One day I missed visualizing this statement and I got a speeding ticket. From that day onwards I have never missed visualizing this statement. I visualize my vision statement first thing in the morning (more on vision statement later).

I have another vision statement, "I'm a genius and I apply my wisdom". Now you can write whatever vision statement you want and start visualizing everyday. Let's say you are going for a job interview, your vision statement for that day could be, "I have a job". Visualize yourself passing the interview and getting the job.
Now you have the **"ABC of SUCCESS"** in your hands. Achieve whatever you want in your life by following the steps outlined.

A = AIM for it. It could be short term, mid term or long term. Write your Vision statements (what you want to be) in the present, achieved form and with the end result in sight.

B = BELIEVE in YOURSELF and believe in what you are doing. The sky is the limit.
C = CONCEIVE (Visualize daily with all of your six senses).
Let us start writing our vision statements and start visualizing right now. You know if you say later, later never comes.

VISION STATEMENTS:

—

—

—

"Whatever your mind can conceive and believe, it can also achieve through positive mental **ATTITUDE**."
- Clement Stone

“When you do not go within, you go without.”
- Author Unknown

“Behind every successful person, there is always somebody who says, “I went to school with him/her.” Why not be that successful person?”

“Life is 10% of what happens to you, and 90% of how you respond to it.”
- Author Unknown

Chapter 1

BURNING DESIRE

"Hopes never come true,
Wishes once in a while come true,
Dreams seldom come true,
Burning Desires always come true,"

Have a Burning Desire to achieve your goal. A **Burning Desire** TO **Be** and TO **Do** is the starting point of all great achievements. Then **'Have'** comes by itself. Remember the **BE-DO-HAVE** Formula. Make your desire the obsession of your life.

Henry Ford had a burning desire to produce a V-8 motor. He told his engineers to produce it. They replied, "It is impossible to do." But Henry said, "Produce it anyway." He told them to stay on the job until they produced it no matter how much time was required. Six months went by with nothing happening. Another six months were gone and still nothing happened. The engineers tried every possible and conceivable way to carry out his order but it looked impossible. Henry said again, "I want it and I will have it." They went ahead again to fulfill his Burning Desire and the secret was discovered. The impossible was turned into the possible by the power of BURNING DESIRE.

"A Daring Successful Attempt By An Exiled Person To Rescue His Family"

In 1992, an exiled person was in America and his wife and two boys were left behind in Cuba. He wanted his family to leave Cuba, but the Cuban Government would not let them leave the country. He approached the Presidents of both the U.S.A. and RUSSIA to intervene and let his family out, but with no results. Finally he borrowed $30,000 to buy a small plane. He sent a message to his family to come to a particular beach in Cuba on a certain day and he would pick them up. He flew from Florida to the beach in Cuba where his family was waiting for him and rescued them out of the country. What a daring act. That is the power of BURNING DESIRE.

Let us take an example. If a person did not eat anything for a week, he would be starving. He would have a BURNING DESIRE to eat anything he could find. He would surely find something to eat because he would be really hungry. In a similar way, when you make yourself really hungry for your GOAL, you will have Burning Desire to achieve it, no matter what. Think of when you were young and in LOVE. In spite of obstacles, you will find the way to meet your loved one because you have Burning Desire with passion.

In 1985, I was a contract Manager for CIA (it's not what you think, CIA stands for "Combined Insurance of America). I had a BURNING DESIRE to sell over 100 accident and sickness policies to get the HALL OF FAME award. My goal was to sell 105 policies. Guess what, I sold exactly 105 policies in a week.

Then in 1988 I sold 112 life insurance policy units in a week to get another HALL OF FAME award from CIA. I got the hall of fame because that was the pre-condition for the management contract and my BURNING DESIRE was to get the management contract.

Let us do an exercise, 'You WANT To' versus 'You HAVE to'.

Make a daily "To Do" list for a particular day and then divide the list into two parts, the things you HAVE to do and the things you WANT to do. Then study what happened next day. You will feel guilty if you missed anything from your 'Have To' list, but you will not regret if you missed anything from your 'Want To' list. You can see the power of 'Have To'. Therefore, whenever you want to achieve something, say that you "HAVE TO rather than you "WANT TO".

Let me share with you another story of BURNING DESIRE and WILL POWER. Do you remember Wilma Rudolph the great Olympic athlete who was born premature and weighed only 4.5 pounds. She was bedridden as she battled double pneumonia, scarlet fever and polio. She lost the use of her left leg at the age of six and was fitted with leg braces. At the age of 16 she was only a sophomore in high school, but she won a bronze medal at the Olympics Games in Melbourne, Australia. Then in the 1960 Rome Olympics Wilma Rudolph became "the fastest woman in the world."

When interviewed about her success, Wilma said, "My mother taught me very early to believe I could achieve any accomplishment I wanted to. The first was to walk without braces."

She also said, "The most important aspect is to be yourself and have confidence in yourself . . . Triumph cannot be had without a struggle."

Look at the story of Daniel "Rudy" Ruettiger.
He was the son of an oil refinery worker and third of 14 children. He suffered from dyslexia. It took years of determination to overcome obstacles, yet Rudy achieved his first dream to attend Notre Dame and play football for the Fighting Irish. Now he is one of the most popular motivational speakers in the U.S.A.

SIX STEPS TO TURN DESIRE INTO REALITY

Remember the "BE- DO-HAVE" Formula

1. Decide what you want to BE. Have a clear VISION.
2. Find out where you are?
3. Recognize somebody who is already there and relate it to yourself (Mentoring).
4. Get the knowledge you need.

5. Take action - start right NOW!
6. Daily Visualization with all six senses.

"BURNING DESIRE WITH VISUALIZATION PRODUCES ENERGY BY WHICH POSITIVE RESULTS ARE ACCUMULATED"

Let us start writing our Burning Desire. My Burning Desire is to teach people to apply the power of VISION to achieve whatever they want in their lives.

Write your desire list, the things you HAVE to have, for example a new car, a new home, new husband/wife, a new business etc. Think big.

Shakespeare once wrote, "Seize what is highest and you will find what is in between."

ACTION PLAN

My BURNING DESIRE is as follows:

1.

2.

3.

"You must go after your wish. As soon as you start to pursue a dream, your life wakes up and everything has meaning."
- Barbara Sher
Author of "I Could Do Anything If I Only Knew What It Was"

Chapter 2

FORMULA FOR SUCCESS

(ATTITUDE)

There is a saying, "Behind every successful man, there is a woman." Similarly, behind every successful person, there is an **ATTITUDE**.

Attitude can make you or an attitude can break you.

William James, referred to as the father of American psychology, said, "The greatest discovery in my generation is that human beings can alter their life by altering the **ATTITUDE** of their mind.

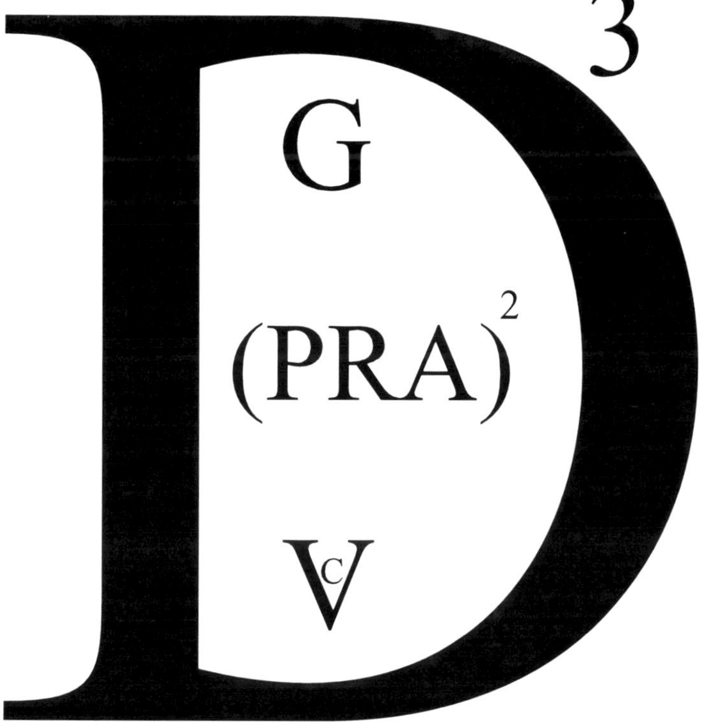

I have a simple way for you to remember this Formula. G = Good, (PRA)2 = POSITIVE RIGHT ATTITUDE twice will bring CV = CASH VALUE and 3D = DIVIDENDS in your LIFE thrice.

G= GOAL
P= Positive Mental Attitude
P= Perception
R = Recognize
R = Relate
A = Assimilate
A = Action
C = Charisma
V = Visualize
D = Desire
D = Dedication
D = Determination

GOAL

The first part of this formula is Goal (G). You must make your daily, short-term and long-term conceivable, achievable and believable goals to succeed in life. After setting handwritten and definite goals, put all your energy, willpower and efforts to achieve those goals. These goals involve a plan you expect to carry out to achieve your main goal. Students, mothers, husbands, wives, engineers, doctors, factory workers, in fact everyone should have goals. The sooner you realize the necessity of setting definite written goals and begin putting all your energy into them, the sooner good things will start to happen to you.

PMA (Positive Mental Attitude)

Self-made millionaire, Clement Stone once said, "Whatever the mind of man can conceive and believe, it can also achieve through PMA." Therefore the most important step is to develop a positive mental attitude. Never refer to any situation as a problem. It's better to refer to it as a challenge. By calling it a challenge instead of a problem, you are developing a positive life attitude. PMA is a winner's attitude. Therefore, to be a winner, you must have a PMA and a PLA (Positive Life Attitude) and then you will be on your way to having the success you MUST have.

PERCEPTION

The next step is to perceive every situation in a positive way. Positive perception produces energy by which positive results are achieved.

RECOGNIZE

To recognize is to identify the principal, idea or technique being used by successful people and begin to use it yourself. If it worked for them, it will work for you.

RELATE

To relate is to connect, to establish relationship. You must relate the success principle to yourself. Start with the most important living person as far as you are concerned – that person is YOU!

ASSIMILATE

To assimilate is to make similar, to incorporate, to absorb, to become a part of those success principles. Find out how you can use these principles to achieve your goals. Absorb the principles to your behavior so that they become a part of you. Develop a success habit. Success begets success, so do not worry, the right thing will automatically start happening for you.

ACTION

Action means to denote, use and to follow-through by applying the principles of successful people. Ask yourself these important questions:
When am I going to use it?
When am I going to start?

Follow the self-starting motivator: DO IT NOW! DO IT NOW! DO IT NOW!

CHARISMA

According to an expert, charisma is defined as “that personal magic that makes people like you and respect you.” It is a quality that anyone can develop by following a few simple steps (see Chapter 7).

VISUALIZATION

Make visualization a part of your life. Visualize everything you do in your life by conceiving it happening in your mind, in an achieved way, the way you want. See how your life will be changed for the better. It is a powerful tool. Nothing comes true, unless you make a picture of it. More on visualizations see Chapter 4.

DESIRE

The next most important thing is a desire. I call it a burning desire because if you do not make it a burning desire, chances are you will not achieve it. Have a burning desire for whatever you have to do.

DETERMINATION

Self-confidence and determination is the key to success. Make a firm determination of your goals. Follow a win-or-perish attitude. Do not look back. Burn the bridge behind you.

DEDICATION

The final key is dedication. Dedicate yourself one hundred percent to achieve your goals.
Now you can apply the formula, "Good positive right attitude twice will bring cash value and dividends in your life thrice" to achieve the happiness, success and health you have to have.

"John was so busy learning the trick of the trade, he forgot to learn the trade."

"I think what I represent is achieving what you want in life. It's a matter of your attitude. Some people have a negative attitude, and that's their disability."

- Marla Runyan

Legally blind U.S. 1,500M Olympic hopeful

Chapter 3

VISUALIZATION

"A PERSON WITHOUT A VISION MAY NEVER FIND A GOOD LIFE."

You can achieve great success by starting to apply VISUALIZATION in your life because VISUALIZATION activates the creative power of your subconscious mind. You can develop this natural power and apply it correctly for your immediate benefit. When you learn to use the power of creative visualization, there is no reason why you should not be fulfilling all your desires.

Visualization is very powerful and an extraordinary phenomenon available to everyone. You can use it or lose it. It releases energy by which positive results are achieved. It works. As Claude M. Bristol writes in his famous book, The Magic of Believing, "The person with a clear goal, a clear picture of his desire, or an ideal always before him, causes it, through repetition, to be buried deeply in his subconscious mind and is thus enabled, thanks to the generative and sustaining power, to realize his goal in a minimum of time and with a minimum of physical effort."

All you have to do is to close your eyes, make a mental picture and see your goal as already complete using all your six senses. That is all Visualization is. It is very simple.

According to an old Hindu legend; at one time, all men and women on earth were gods, but those men and women so sinned and abused the DIVINE POWER that Brahma, the god of all gods, decided that godhead should be taken away from human beings and hidden somewhere where they should never again find it to abuse it.

"We will bury it deep in the earth." said the other gods.

"No," said Brahma, "Because man will

dig down in the earth and find it."
"Then we will sink it in the deepest ocean." They said.
"No," said Brahma, "Because man will learn to dive and find it there too."
"We will hide it on the highest mountain" They said.
"No," said Brahma, "Because man will someday climb every mountain on the earth and again capture the godhead."
"Then we do not know where to hide it, where she/he cannot find it." Said the other gods.
"I will tell you." Said Brahma.

"HIDE IT DOWN INSIDE MEN AND WOMEN. HE/SHE WILL NEVER THINK TO LOOK THERE."

And that is what they did. Hidden down inside every man and woman is some of the **DIVINE POWER**. Ever since then men and women have gone over the earth digging, diving and climbing, looking for that god like quality which all the time is hidden down within themselves. It is this SPARK that I would like you to turn into a blaze - it is this **RADIANCE** we must capture. It is something **GENUINE**, something for everyday use. It is the **SPIRIT** that naturally makes you do the right thing at the right time and can make you really successful in your life. Each of us can use this **DIVINE POWER** by having **PMA**, **MEDITATION** and **VISUALIZATION** to lead us to a life of **SUCCESS**, **WEALTH** and **HAPPINESS**.

You can use creative visualization to:

1. Relax your body
2. Gain confidence.
3. Develop PMLA (Positive Mental Life Attitude)
4. Have an adequate SELF-IMAGE.
5. Become healthy.
6. Improve your relationship with others.

7. Achieve your goals.
8. Quit smoking.
9. Control drinking and many more ways to improve your life.
10. Control weight (Not to lose weight because when you lose something, you will try to find it again).

Whatever you want to achieve, make a mental picture of it in your conscious mind and then start visualizing at least ten times daily. You know the average person uses less than 7% of their brain. If you want to use more, start visualizing everything you do in your life. You will be surprised at your mind's amazing potential.

Think of a beautiful garden. The gardener has to sow seeds to get flowers and he also has to take care of the garden to get beautiful flowers. You know "As you sow, so shall you reap." Our thoughts are just like the seeds. If you want a beautiful life, you have to sow beautiful seeds (THOUGHTS) by visualizing a

'Beautiful Life'.
When we have PMLA (Positive Mental Life Attitude), we tend to get happiness and the things we want. On the other hand, when we have NMLA (Negative Mental Life Attitude), we are negative, fearful and insecure and tend to attract negative situations and people that we do not like.
When we are using creative visualization, we are programming our mind/brain bio-computer. Your brain is hardware (an actual computer). Your mind is software (the programs) and you are the **Programmer.**

The brain has approximately thirty billion neurons, just like the components of the computer. You are born with approximately two thousands programs in your mental computer that are designed to run your body perfectly. The programs store your experiences and learning and feed this information back to you on demand. When we get older, our programs start to become defective because of the accumulated stress in our life.

For example, a few days after you are born, your mother suddenly disappeared out of your sight, you were hungry and there was no food. That is stress. Our life is controlled by our significant others, parents, teachers, relatives etc. We do things to make them happy without caring for ourselves, giving more stress to ourselves. With more and more stress our perfect programs start to become imperfect. Our organs and essential systems of the body start to function less and we start using less of our brain. You can start using more of your brain by starting CREATIVE VISUALIZATION. Your vision statements are like new programs for your bio-computer.

Let us say you are going for a job interview. Before the interview, visualize at least five times. You will see the impact. Because your brain sees no difference between actually happening or visualizing. Your vision statement should be, “I have passed the job interview.” Make a mental picture of it – you are in the interview and you are passing the interview.

Harvard University researchers have found that those students, who visualized in advance performed tasks with nearly 100% accuracy while students who did not visualize achieved only 55% accuracy. Almost all Olympic and professional athletes now use the power of VISUALIZATION.

Let us look at the story of Evelyn Monahan. She was involved in a serious accident in the 1960s. As a result of a bad head injury, she became blind. Her doctors told her that she could not be cured. She was 22 years young with no sight. She also became an epileptic having dozens of seizures each day. A few years later she suffered another accident, which paralyzed her right arm. After finding out her conventional treatment had not worked, she tried to find different ways. She found **Visualization** Techniques. She tried the techniques. After 10 days, her eyesight returned and her seizures stopped. Her doctors found no further evidence of epilepsy and were amazed. Even she started moving her right arm freely. See the power of Visualization.

According to an article in the *Kitchener-Waterloo Record* on December 8, 1989, “Roughriders had a psychological edge in winning the Grey Cup.” Glen Suiter of the Roughriders believed the power of the mind (Visualization) had a lot to do with the Roughriders winning the Grey Cup in 1989 in a 43-40 Canadian Football League masterpiece over the Hamilton Tiger Cats. They kept it secret until they won the Grey Cup. They became 89ers in their hearts & in their minds (by visualizing).

Let me share with you another story of the power of visualization. A woman wanted to buy a farm-house. She drove around the area and found a house similar to her choice. She took a picture of the house, went home and started doing daily visualization for getting the house of her choice. After some time she found the house and bought it. When she was taking possession of the house, she found a piece of junk (a very old tractor) in the yard. She was not pleased. She called her agent and told him to get the junk removed from the yard. The agent told her that she bought the property as it is and therefore he was not able to do anything. She was really mad because she bought her very expensive dream home but a piece of junk came with it. When she examined the picture of the house she used to visualize to get her dream home, there was an old tractor in the yard in the picture. She was amazed with the power of visualization because she received the piece of junk with the expensive house.

Whenever you want something, get a complete description of the thing before starting visualization. Let us say you want a new car. Go for a test drive in that car and take a picture of you sitting inside. Then start visualizing daily.

Vision Statements should be phrased in the present tense and in achieved form. Never use words like will, not etc.

Let us look at some examples:

1. I am calm and confident.
2. I always have healthy body and mind.
3. All of my investments are profitable.
4. I have a great day.
5. I have excellent relationships with my family and friends.
6. I am increasing my wealth.
7. My monthly income is always more than my expenses.
8. I have a positive mental attitude.
9. I am a very energetic person.
10. I am always a happy person.
11. I am always successful.
12. I am a slim person. (Visualize yourself the way you want to look)
13. I am the best student in the class.
14. I have rid myself of my smoking habits. (Visualize yourself without smoking)
15. I am the best basketball player in the school.

Now let us do a **VISUALIZATION** exercise:

1. Sit in a comfortable chair or lay down in a comfortable quiet place.
2. Take a deep breath three times, inhaling through the nose and exhaling through the mouth, relaxing all your body parts from head to foot.
3. Count backwards slowly from 31 to 1 and picture yourself on the top of a set of stairs going to your ideal place of relaxation (it could be a beach, a beautiful garden etc). When you count as you go down the stairs, use your six senses, (your sixth sense is your creative imagination). When you are going down the stairs, feel there are lemon trees around the stairs and smell the aroma of the lemon trees.
4. When you reach the number 1, project yourself into your ideal place of relaxation.
5. Say to yourself mentally, whatever it is you have to have: "I have a great

day, today", "I am a slim person", "I am very confident"; "I have a good memory"; "I Have quit smoking"; "I have a new car'; "I have a new home" etc.

You can come out of this state by just counting from 1 to 7.

It is the best to start your day with daily VISUALIZATION. Because your thoughts during the first thirty-one minutes after you wake up will greatly influence your day ahead. Think of peace and happiness during this time period. By controlling your morning thoughts, you can control your day ahead. Once you say to yourself in a calm earnest way statements like the following:
I have a great day today.
I am calm and cool today.
I am very happy today.

You will see the difference. On the other hand if you start your morning with bitterness, worry and depression, you are subject to a day of misfortunes and discords.

Now let us start writing our Vision Statements:

1.

2.

3.

4.

5.

6.

7.

8.

"They tell you will lose your mind when you grow older, but they don't tell is that you won't miss it very much."
- Malcolm Cowley

"Be wiser than other people if you can, but do not tell them so."
- Philip Stanhope, Earl of Chesterfield

"It is what is in your head that determines what is in your hand."
Robert T. Kiyosaki

"There was a brain being auctioned in Russia. One brain had belonged to a Russian scientist and the other one belonged to an illiterate person. Guess which one received the highest bid? It was the one that belonged to the illiterate person. Why? Because it had never been used."

"A person went for a brain surgery. After the surgery the doctor forgot to put back his brain. He went home and started working. After a week when the hospital noticed that he left the brain behind, he was called to come back and get his brain. When he came back, the doctor asked him, "How did you do your job for a week without a brain." He answered, " I do not need the brain to do my job."

Chapter 4

GOALS

"A MAN WITHOUT A GOAL IS LIKE A BOAT WITHOUT A RUDDER"

In 1954, Yale University graduating seniors were asked if they had SPECIFIC WRITTEN GOALS at the time of graduation. Only 3% had done so while approximately 10% had SPECIFIC GOALS but had not committed them to paper and 85% had NO specific goals. In 1974, twenty years later, these same people were surveyed again. The 3% outperformed the other 97% combined, FINANCIALLY, SPIRITUALLY AND PERSONALLY!

According to another study, 27% of people never think of goals, 60% gave some thought to goals, another 10%

thought well of goals but only 3% had **definite** and **written** goals.

We are like a ship leaving port without having the slightest idea of where we want to go. Most of us are too lost to achieve our goals in our life.
YOU have the potential to get whatever you want in your life as long as you are not addicted to the "HOPEium" drug (Hope-hope-hope). Did you know that only "HAP" (Hope And Pray) people are addicted to this drug? When you have a burning desire and will power, you can achieve whatever you want in your life by having conceivable, achievable and believable goals. There is nothing magic about success. What it requires is a focused effort and a plan of action after setting your goals.
There are three different kinds of goals as follows:

1. Daily goals.
2. Short-term goals, up to two years.
3. Long-term goals, two to five years.

There are also six different categories of goals as follows:

1. Family
2. Financial
3. Business
4. Recreational
5. Health
6. Humanitarian

TEN STEPS TO GOAL ACHIEVEMENT

1. Have a BURNING DESIRE and WILL POWER to achieve your goals, not because you want to, but you HAVE to.
2. You must BELIEVE that you can achieve your goals.
3. Ask yourself the question, "WHAT'S IN IT FOR ME and why do I want to achieve this goal." List the reasons.
4. Set a TARGET DATE for achieving the goals.

5. Identify obstacles and FIND SOLUTIONS to overcome them.
6. Get the KNOWLEDGE you are going to need.
7. Identify the PEOPLE whose cooperation and support you are going to need. Support can come from a spouse, friends, business associates or a significant other. Share your goals with these people who share in your commitment.
8. Prepare a PLAN OF ACTION. List the activities, like writing sub-goals and measuring the progress.
9. Write AFFIRMATIONS and VISUALIZE daily, ex. "I am a confident and successful person."
10. Always BACKUP your plan with three D's: "Determination, Dedication and Desire". Never give up. Remember, "Winners never quit and quitters never win."

"Where there is a will, there is a way."

Let's start writing your goals right now. First write the list of the things, you are not happy with. Then write the things you want to change and those will be your goals.

FAMILY GOALS

(For example, getting a life partner)

Rank Goal Target Date

1.

2.

3.

FINANCIAL GOALS

(For example, Income of $5000 per month)

Rank Goal Target Date

1.

2.

3.

BUSINESS GOALS

(For example, starting a new business)

Rank	Goal	Target Date
1.		
2.		
3.		

RECREATIONAL GOALS

(For Example, starting a new hobby)

Rank	Goal	Target Date
1.		
2.		
3.		

HEALTH GOALS

(For example, getting rid of high blood pressure)

Rank	Goal	Target Date
1.		
2.		
3.		

HUMANITY GOALS

(For example, starting a Volunteer job)

Rank	Goal	Target Date
1.		
2.		
3.		

"Goals are stepping stones and a simple secret to success."

"Goals can make you happy, healthy and wealthy."

G = Getting
O = OUTSTANDING
A = ACHIEVEMENT in
L = LIFE

"The trouble with a mental goal is that the ink fades so fast."

"A well-written life is almost as rare as a well-spent one."

- Thomas Carlyle

Chapter 5

ACTION

You know there are three kinds of people in the world as follow:

1. Those who watch what is happening;
2. Those who wonder what is happening;
3. Those who make things happen – **Action People.**

I am sure you are the third kind otherwise you would not be reading this book. In case you are one of the other types of people, please convert yourself into an ACTION person to be successful.

"Lack of action is the most dangerous thing"

I use a motivator, "Do it now or there may be a law against it later."

1. First of all, make a list of "**Things** I am **not happy with**" for each category of goals.
2. Then make a list of **"Things I want to change"**.
3. Make an **"I want" list** (Completely describe what you truly want).
4. Turn this list into an "I **MUST HAVE" list**.
5. Turn this into a vision statement.

Let us take an example of a goal of having to need a new car.

1. **Things you are not happy list** – First find the reason why you want a new car. It could be you have an old car you are not happy with it or you are taking a bus.
2. **Things to Change list** – Then you want to change the old car to a new car.
3. **Want list** – I want a new car. Get a complete description. For example: Jeep liberty SUV-2005 fully loaded.

1. **Must have list** – "I must have a brand new SUV Jeep Liberty fully loaded 2005."
2. **Vision statement** – "I have a brand new jeep liberty fully loaded 2005 SUV."
3. Start doing your daily **visualization**.

Repeat the same steps for each goal. You will see the power of visualization yourself.

When you achieve your goal, always reward yourself. You know the meaning of **"WIIFM"** (What is in it for me?)

Now let us go back to your **family goals**.

Write the **things you are not happy with**.

1.

2.

3.

4.

5.

Things you want to change list

1.
2.
3.
4.
5.

I want list

1.
2.
3.
4.
5.

I have to have list

1.
2.
3.
4.

Vision Statement

1.

2.

3.

4.

5.

Do the same thing with all other categories of goals. Then you should have a list of all of your **Vision Statements (GOALS)**. I have ten statements in my list. I call it – **My Ten Commandments of SUCCESS**. Everybody will have different numbers of statements. It does not matter how many you have in your list. Once you have this list, make it part and parcel of your life. This is your blue print for your life. You can make amendments to this list whenever you feel it is necessary.

Here is an example to show you why you should keep this list with you all the time. At 1996 Olympics in Atlanta, Olympic decathlon gold medallist Bruce Jenner asked a roomful of Olympic participants if they had a list of written goals, everybody raised their hands. Then he asked how many of them had their list with them right that time and only one person raised his hand. Guess who this person was. He was Dan O'Brien and he went on to win the gold medal in the decathlon in the 1996 Olympics. See the power of having written goal statements with you all the time?

Now all you have to do daily is to Visualize as many times as possible. The more times you visualize, the faster you get the results. Start visualizing five times a day, then ten times and so on. It is best to do at least twenty times a day. Once you memorize your vision statement it does not take long. I visualize each statement five times at a time - four times daily. I begin with the first statement in the list and visualize it five times. Then I do the same thing with the remaining nine statements. It takes me less than five minutes. Then I repeat this whenever convenient. I also repeat this just before I go to sleep. Do it with all six senses.

First thing in the morning, I also visualize: SITUATION + REACTION = OUTCOME. Think of the situations you are going to face in the day ahead. Visualize each situation in a positive way. You are going to be amazed at the results. Remember **OUTCOME** is the result of your **REACTION** to the **SITUATION**. You can change the outcome by reacting in a positive way.

"Even if you are on the right track, you'll get run over if you just sit there."

"In order to help her employees to stop procrastination, the president of the company hung up signs throughout the building that said, "Do it now." Within 24 hours, her assistant quit, her secretary ran away with her boyfriend, and the security guard stole her B.M.W."

Chapter 6

CHARISMA

Some people are more successful than others in their lives, not because they are more educated, intelligent and talented, but because they have **CHARISMA**. Any body can develop this quality. It can build self-confidence and self-esteem. In this chapter, you are going to learn to enhance this personal magnetism with a very simple formula. You will become ENTHUSIASTIC, OPTIMISTIC and ENERGETIC. I call this the **"CASH"** formula, which is as follows:

C = Compliment
A = Argument
S = Smile
H = Hospitality

Compliment: Give at least 1 to 3

sincere compliments a day to the people in your daily life and see how your life will change for the better. Be a caring person. Be concerned for others. Compromise with others. This will lead you to develop this magnetic personality.

Argument: Never argue with other people. Give your point of view and be firm. Be **accountable** for your actions. Develop a positive **Attitude**. Pay **attention** to other people and their needs. There is an old saying:

"Never start an argument over the dinner table as a half filled stomach generates more heat."

Smile: Always smile. When you smile at strangers, they usually smile back at you. When you cry, nobody cries with you, but when you smile, everybody smiles with you. Be **sincere** to others.

Hospitality: Develop the habit of hospitality and you will see how people like you more. Be **humorous**.

These are the following benefits of developing **CHARISMA**:

1. Improve and strengthen your relationship with others.
2. Become more successful in your business and life.
3. Turn destructive criticism into constructive criticism (positive)
4. Develop self-esteem.
5. Develop self-confidence.
6, Develop positive attitude.
7. Develop vision in your life.
8. Become more comfortable with strangers.
9. Inspire others.
10. Influence others.
11. Become likeable by others.
12. Make sincere and interesting long life friends.
13. Work to achieve your goals.
14. Develop good comfortable working environment.
15. Help people to become positive.
16. Develop a positive self-image.
17. Earn higher income.

18. Close more and bigger sales.
19. Find and attract a romantic partner.
20. Get promoted more easily.
21. Escape being laid off or downsized.
22. Get elected to office.
23. Become more enthusiastic.
24. Get more sincere compliments.
25. People do more things for you.
26. Uplift others.
27. Become more effective.
28. Take sensible and calculated risks.
29. Control situations.
30. Get attention from people and become recognized.
31. Promote yourself.

Let us start using this CASH formula daily to develop Charisma. You will see the results yourself. Remember to do it now. Write the things on the lists you want to achieve by developing **Charisma** and using this trait.

Action Plan:

1.

2.

3.

4.

5.

Chapter 7

MEDITATION

"Meditation is a great thing,
Its star is soaring,
Close your eyes and
Do silent recitation,
Think deep,
Not fair if,
You start snoring."

Meditation is the key to a healthy body. Healthy body creates a healthy mind. When we have a healthy mind we can achieve whatever we want. Let us first look at the benefits of Meditation. Why should we do meditation? Most of us do not have enough mind power to deal with daily conflicts and that is why there are so many problems in the world. When we sleep we build natural mind power but that is not enough to deal with daily life problems like problems at work, driving problems etc. When we do not have enough sleep we can hardly gain mind power. You can see why we are restless the next day because of lack of mind power.

Benefits of Meditation:

1. Increases mind power.
2. Promotes sound sleep.
3. Leads to extraordinary happiness.
4. Gets rid of Anxiety.
5. Better Health - Eliminates illnesses.
6. Helps develop ESP.
7. Reduces stress.
8. Reduces anger.
9. Brightens wisdom.
10. Provides energy.
11. Promotes carefulness.
12. Helps to develop a gentle mind.
13. Helps to develop a positive mental attitude.
14. Promotes well-being.
15. Restrains cruelty.
16. Provides good fortune.
17. Helps to develop decent feelings.
18. Reduces mistakes.
19. Develops charisma.

20. Creates humaneness towards others.
21. Promotes world peace.
22. Strengthens courage.
23. Improves problem-solving skills.
24. Develops greater relaxation.
25. Develops selflessness.
26. Promotes peace of mind and calmness.
27. Promotes self-confidence.
28. Promotes self-esteem.
29. Helps us to develop will power.
30. Nurtures intelligence.
31. Develops healing power.
32. Increases human potential.
33. Improves judgement.
34. Promotes consideration.
35. Helps to develop concentration.
36. Promotes accountability.
37. Promotes responsibility.
38. Detaches us from materialism.
39. Reduces jealousy.
40. Produces a better life.
41. Promotes use of more of our brain.
42. Helps us perform better deeds.
43. Reduces blood pressure.
44. Brightens our life outlook.

45. Reduces mental depression.
46. Makes us more persistent.
47. Helps us to develop determination.
48. Promotes dedication.
49. Helps to control our fears.
50. Develops self-control.
51. Promotes discipline.
52. Promotes visualization.
53. Helps to achieve goals.
54. Promotes unity.
55. Benefits society.
56. Provides pain relief.
57. Inspires creativity.
58. Improves coping skills.
59. Encourages more complete remissions.

When we do not do meditation it is like stealing money from yourself. You are committing mental suicide (depleting your mind power). You have to keep building mind power to be wealthy in mind power. When you start doing meditation you will see the benefits.

.

Now let us see how to meditate. Thanks to the Will Power Institute for teaching me their 'Meditation Instructor Course,' which taught me how to teach meditation to other people. It will take only 15 minutes a day and it will not affect your routine activities. There are various ways to do meditation, but I prefer the walking and sitting as follow:

Walking Meditation:

Walking is essential because it promotes good physical and mental health, blood circulation and digestion. You can specify your own distance 5 to 10 meters or even more. You should not move your arms while meditating because motion interferes with tranquility.

First of all, choose a focal point (a point where your mind will focus while meditating). It could be anywhere from the forehead to the navel or your nose, chest, bosom, etc. The forehead is quite a common focal point and is the one I use. Now choose your silent recitation, which

is essential to control and eliminate emotions. It could be: “Buddho”, “Allah”, “Jesus”, “Om” etc. I use “Buddho”. It means “Pure and awaken” the mind.
Now place your right hand over the left and over the abdomen. Focus on your focal point and start silent recitation and start walking very slowly with the right foot first and keep repeating your silent recitation. Walk over the specified distance, stop walking for a moment and turn around from the right and walk back. Repeat the same process for 5-15 minutes.

Sitting Meditation:

It is good to do a walking meditation before the sitting meditation. It will enhance meditation in the sitting position. Sit with your right leg crossed over the left leg, the right hand over the left hand with both palms upwards and sit straight. You can also sit with both legs folding to one side of the body if you find it more comfortable. Sitting on a chair with both legs on the floor is also fine. Start silent recitation while focusing on your focal point. Do it for 5-15 minutes at a time.

Walking Over Cobblestones Meditation:

There is another kind of meditation we are studying called, 'Walking over cobblestones meditation'. Behavioral researchers from the Oregon Research institute investigated the health effects of cobblestones after observing people exercising and walking back and forth over traditional stone paths in China. The path to better health and lower blood pressure may be paved with cobblestones. A study showed that when people over 60 walked on smooth, rounded cobblestones for just a half-hour a day over four months, they significantly lowered their blood pressure and improved their balance. The results surprised Dr. Fisher and his fellow researchers, who expected to see some general improvement in health but also saw blood pressure dropped measurably among the volunteers during the 16-week study.

Cobblestone walking paths are common in China where traditional medicine teaches that the uneven surface of the stones stimulates “acupoints” on the soles of the feet. The theory is much like acupuncture suggesting that distant and unrelated areas of the body are linked together at certain points and can be stimulated to improve physical and mental health. Fay Horak, an Oregon Health and Science University neurophysiologist who specializes in balance, said the study is evidence that finding ways to maintain mobility and balance can delay and even prevent the effects of aging. The researchers in Eugene simulated the rounded river rock cobblestones with a specially designed mat that was 6 feet long and 1? feet wide. Some of the test subjects walked in their bare feet while others wore socks. I have 2 of those mats and I am doing my walking meditation on them. You can also do walking meditation over cobblestones and let me know the results.

MEDITATION ACTION PLAN:

"What appears to be of benefit are the spiritual attitudes"

and

"Spirituality can be as simple as believing in higher purpose or expressing ones faith in daily affirmations, meditation or prayer."

and

"Recovery from depression is like recovery from any major illness"

– Dr. Arun Ravindran, Head of the mood and anxiety disorders program at the center for Addiction and Mental Health at the University of Toronto.

Chapter 8

LIFE MANAGEMENT

"Affirmative visualization with belief in yourself produces energy by which positive results are accumulated."

"Believe in yourself, have full faith, have written goals and do daily visualization with focus, you will get success."

Bill Brick was in Vancouver and he wanted to go to Calgary. He went to the bus terminal and bought the ticket. Having a few minutes to spare, he stepped on a kind of scale and inserted the loonie and here came his fortune, "Your name is Bill Brick, you weigh 160 lbs and you are catching 7:20 to Calgary." He was amazed because all the information was correct. Then he inserted another loonie and here came his fortune again, "You

name is still Bill Brick, you still weigh 160 lbs and you are still catching 7:20 to Calgary". He was more than puzzled. Sensing a trick, he went to the washroom, changed his clothes. He inserted his last loonie, stepped on the scale and here came his fortune again, "Your name is still Bill Brick, you still weigh 160 lbs and you have just missed your 7:20 to Calgary".
This book is for those people, who are missing their 7:20 to Calgary. They are too busy to achieve success. They are not focussed & they have no vision in their life. Once you have a vision & you focus on that, you will achieve whatever you want in your life.

People do not plan to fail but they fail to plan. You know there are two kinds of people as follow:

1. Those who plan before they do anything; and,
2. Those who do things first, and then they plan what to do when it is too late.

Sadly, most of us are in the second category, we do things first and then wonder what happened. It is too late to make your plan after the action has taken place.

Are you the first kind or the second kind? If you are the first kind then congratulations. If you are the second kind **it is time to change**.

Do what most people do not do and you will be successful. You know that most people do not have written goals, do not visualize and do not plan before their action. Therefore to be successful, let us start writing goals, visualizing daily and make plans before we act. You will see the incredible results your self.

Start believing in yourself. Then have a **burning desire** with **faith** and **start visualizing** your goals at least three times a day especially first thing in the morning and at night before bedtime because you are most relaxed at those times and your subconscious mind is most receptive Do **organized planning. Be persistent**. Then the sky is the limit.

Develop more mind power through **meditation** so that you can protect yourself against all negative suggestions and discouraging influences of relatives, friends and acquaintances

Make a **friendly alliance** with one or more persons who will encourage and help you achieve your goals. You should be accountable to that alliance. Remember, "A kiss is a pleasant reminder that two heads are better than one." Organize a mastermind group to help each other.

Anger, greed, fear and jealousy are our worst enemies that prevent us from achieving our success. Therefore get rid of those emotions. You know anger could be dealt three different ways as follow:

1. By expressing explosively – which is not an effective method as you are hurting yourself. When you are angry

you lose energy and this is not helpful. Just let it go by not reacting. Be **proactive**.

2. By suppressing your anger. Suppression is not good either because you will be more stressed and this will also make you lose energy.
3. By staying cool from the energy you acquired **through meditation**. **Let it go**. Just think that those people who try to make you angry are insane.

"Anger is stupidity, fury is madness. If you do not succumb to anger, you will not succumb to stupidity and madness."
- Phra Phayom Kalayano

You know what FEAR stands for: False Expectations Appearing Real. Ninety percent of the time your fear does not come true and the 10% will not help anyway, then why exhibit fear.
Same with your worries, most never

materialize and you worry for nothing. There is an old saying, "One does not live for even a hundred years yet he/she worries enough for thousands".

"The reason why worry kills more people than work is that more people worry than work."
- Robert Frost

Therefore quit worrying and start visualizing.
Jealousy is like a poison. It will hurt you and the other person. Then why be jealous.
Greed looks good in the beginning, but in the end, it will get you down. Then why be greedy.
There is another formula I use called the DEP Formula.
D = DISCILPINE: Have discipline in your life.
E = EMOTIONS: Get rid of emotions like greed and fear.
P = PATIENCE: Have patience.

"Anyone can achieve prosperity if they so choose."
- Robert Kiyosaki

In your life when you need more money for something important, never say, "I can't afford it." Your brain stops working to look for more money. Ask yourself, "How can I afford it?" This way your brain is put to work to look for more money. This way you also exercise your brain and it becomes stronger and stronger. There is an old saying, "Use your mind or lose your mind."

"The single most powerful asset we all have is our mind."
- Robert Kiyosaki

You know our life is like a train but usually somebody else is driving it. Our lives are out of our control and in somebody else's hands. Why are we not driving our own train? We should be in control. Our goal is to be in the driver's seat of our lives. We need to observe who the most significant people are and how they are positioned in our lives. Are they standing over us because they feel superior and they are moving forward in their lives and leaving us behind? Is it someone from your past who has dominated you and what you do even though they may not still be present in your life now? Are they taking you where you want to go? Chances are they are not. Remember, "What other people do or say is their stuff and how we react is our stuff." When somebody does something to try to make us angry, we do not have to get mad. If we do get angry we are giving them control of our life. They can make us mad whenever they want. By not reacting to their action we control our own life. So why not take control of your life by taking the action of setting written goals and visualizing daily and start driving your own train.

"Man often becomes what he believes

himself to be. If I keep on saying to myself that I cannot do a certain thing, it is possible that I may end by really becoming incapable of doing it. On the contrary, if I shall have the belief that I can do it, I shall surely acquire the capacity to do it, even if I may not have it at the beginning."

- Mahatma Gandhi
1869–1948, Indian Nationalist Leader

"We all have two great gifts in our life, MIND and TIME. Use them properly and spend MONEY wisely, you will achieve success in your life. Robert T Kiyosaki has well said in his book, Rich Dad Poor Dad, "Spend it foolishly, you choose to be poor. Spend it on liabilties, you join the middle class. Invest it in your mind and learn how to acquire assets and you will be choosing wealth as your goal."

"Become a fearless good student, teacher and sales person, success will be yours."

"A fool and his money is one big party."

"Following the path of least resistance is what makes rivers and men crooked."

"Learn from the mistakes of others. You can't live long enough to make them all yourself."

"One machine can do the work of fifty ordinary men, no machine can do the work of one extraordinary man."
- Elbert Hubbard

"He who teaches often, learns himself."
- Italian Proverb

"Too many people spend money they have not earned, to buy things they do not want to impress people they do not like"
- Will Smith

EPILOGUE: YOU ARE ON YOUR WAY TO SUCCESS

This is not the end but is the beginning of you taking Control of your own life. Remember I told you in the beginning, my daughter went to her friend's house by ACCIDENT. Guess what? She does not do it anymore. Now she goes by CHOICE not by accident. A few years ago I used to live by the LAW OF ACCIDENT. Now I live by the Law of CHOICE. I am sure you have also started living by the law of choice now. If not then let us begin immediately. Then you are controlling your life instead of life controlling you.

There is a saying, " Everybody wants to

go to HEAVEN but nobody wants to die." You cannot go to heaven on your "BUTS" or "IFS" (you know IF stands for INSTANT FAILURE). Let me show you that anybody can go to PARADISE or HEAVEN without dying.

HEAVEN and HELL are on this earth. Both are at the same place. This place is divided by a partition and on one side is heaven and on the other side is hell. When you look at both sides you will not find any difference. Both sides have long tables and the best food. People on both sides have seven-foot long spoons tied to their hands. The people on the hell side can't eat their food because when they try to put the food in their mouths it falls on the floor. You can see that they are in hell because they cannot eat food even if they have the best food. On the other side (PARADISE), people have the same seven-foot long spoons tied to their hand but they are feeding each other. They are in HEAVEN enjoying the best food.

Now you can see the difference between heaven and hell. People helping each other and working together in unity are living in heaven, and the people who are not working as a team live in hell. You want to enjoy heaven then start helping each other. To get food, you have to give food. To get love, you have to give love. Whatever you want to receive you have to give without any expectation of getting back. You will receive more than you gave.

First of all we have to forgive ourselves and every body else for the past. Forgiveness is the best form of revenge. Get rid of the grudges you have against anybody. It will unlock your brakes for the best life you want. Let me share with you an old story.

There were two monks. They started the day with the vow of silence and went around to get the food. There was a river on the way and one beautiful young girl with her party clothes was waiting on the one side of the river. She was scared to cross the river because she did not want to spoil her clothes. One of the monks felt sorry for her. He picked up the girl and dropped her on the other side of the river. The other monk was furious about this because monks are not suppose to touch women. He kept his anger inside until night time when they broke the vow of silence. The first thing he said to the other monk was, "Why did you carry that young girl across the river." The other monk replied, "I have put her away a long time ago. Why are you still carrying her?"

Now let us quickly review everything and call it the ten commandments of success.

1. AIM: Decide what you WANT out of your life. Focus on mission not on commission. Have your handwritten goals with you all the time. Think conceivably big.
2. BELIEVE: Believe in yourself that you are going to achieve your goals.

Have full FAITH.

3. VISUALIZE: Make VISION part and parcel of your life. Visualize everything in your life. It will change your life for the better.
4. ACTION: Do whatever you have to do to achieve your goals.
5. FOCUS: Stay focussed on your aim. Do not loose track.
6. STUDENT: Be a good student and listener. Listening is more important than talking. God has given us only one mouth and two ears. Learning is a life long process. Remember, "Use your mind or lose your mind."
7. TEACHER: Teach everything you know to others. You will get better and better. Now you can teach others to make VISION part and parcel of their lives. Teach at least ten people the art of VISUALIZATION.
8. SALESPERSON: By learning the skills of communicating, negotiating and handling the fear of rejection, your life will become easier.

9. FEARLESS: Get rid of the fear of losing. You know losing inspires winners and defeats losers. When people are scared to lose they surely lose. Failures are the stepping stones to success. Learn from your failures instead of crying.
10. MEDITATION: Do daily meditation. Meditation and prayer is the same thing. Just a different name.

"The main reason that over ninety 90 percent of the American public struggles financially is because they play not to lose. They do not play to win."
- Robert Kiyosaki

Do you have your written Goals handy?
Do you Visualize daily?

If not then let us start right now and please share with me your success stories.

REMEMBER: BE-DO-HAVE
It is all up to YOU.

A young man went to see an old wise woman. He had a small bird hidden in his hands. He assumed that the wise old woman would know about the small bird. The young man asked, "Is the bird dead or alive?" If she said it was dead, he would let the bird go. If she said it was alive, he would crush it to prove her wrong.
The conversation went as follows:
"What is in my hands, madam?" asked the young man.
"A small bird." The wise old woman answered.
He than asked, "Is it dead or alive?"
"My dear," said the wise old woman, "The answer lies in your hands, the bird's life is in your hands, dead or alive."
- Author Unknown

We can learn from this story that our life is in our own hands. Make it or break it. Therefore let us make it the BEST. I have full FAITH in YOU. You have a GENIUS inside you. Let us wake up that GENIUS.

Remember:

ACTION

DO IT NOW
DO IT NOW
DO IT NOW
YOU CAN DO IT.

ACTION

YOU ARE THE GENIUS.

ACTION